THE

HOLY HEART

Holly Garman

En Route Books and Media, LLC

Saint Louis, MO

Make the time

En Route Books and Media, LLC
5705 Rhodes Avenue
St. Louis, MO 63109

Contact us at
contactus@enroutebooksandmedia.com

Cover credit: Holly Garman

ISBN-13: 978-1-956715-15-6

Library of Congress Control Number:
2021952257

Table of Contents

Foreword by Fr. John Horn, S.J....................i

Introduction..1

The Creed of the Holy Heart........................9
Daily Intentions of the Holy Heart...........11

Part 1 – The Promises

Section A..14
Section B..24
Section C..35
Section D..45
Section E..52

Part 2 – The Instructions

Section F..64

Part 3 – The Call

Section G 78

Epilogue 85

Foreword

Images "think," "feel," and engender "desires" within us as we apprehend them. In faith, sacred images "speak" words in silence that penetrate our being. These words heal us to become who we really are as images of God who is Love.

The Holy Heart, by Holly Garman, is an inspirational book that greatly serves to form us and strengthen our faith by giving us access into the hidden meaning and efficacy of a beautiful sacred image that portrays Trinitarian love. The Trinity's own "thoughts," "feelings," and "desires" are unveiled for each of us to taste and see. This is a book that invites us to receive the regenerating creative power of Scripture as the Living Word.

"The Holy Heart" is a sacred image that presents universal truths about the Trinity's relational love. These universal truths are easily applicable to each person's unique personality and history. I believe that personal and institutional renewal flows from this imaginative portrayal of the interior life of the Trinity.

Pray with this book. Listen in silence and permit Jesus, the Father, and the Holy Spirit to love you into new life in particular ways. Respond generously to the Trinity's laboring love that is desiring to communicate with you. Happiness and joy will increase beyond your wildest dreams. Let "receiving" God's love be the measure of your success before "doing" anything. Receiving the presence of God is the most fruitful human activity.

Our praying with this book promises to fill us anew with awe and wonder. After all, we become who and what we contemplate. And, as we contemplate "The Holy Heart" we open ourselves to being surprised again and again in the on-going discovery that we are causing the Trinity's joy (Zeph. 3: 14-18).

Fr. John Horn, S.J.

The Holy Heart

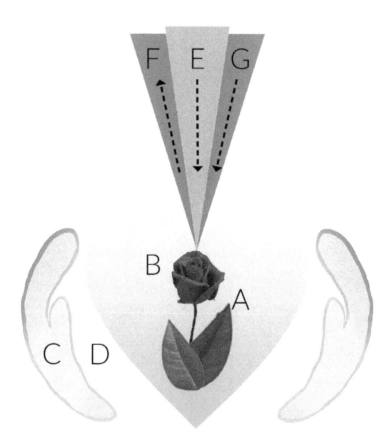

Introduction

On December 4, 2006, I was spending time in prayer when the Lord inspired me to draw the image of what He told me was called The Holy Heart. That day was the one-year anniversary of my father's death, and just a little over one year after I had completed my own treatment for cancer. My journey through diagnosis, surgery, and treatments was one that took me deeper than ever into the Lord's Presence. I had learned and experienced so much.

As I was spending time in prayer that evening, I told God that I didn't want to forget all that He had taught me, and I asked if He would please help me to write it all down in some way so that I could ponder it over time, and He could transform me by His truths. I rose from my seat to leave the room, assuming that at some future point God would inspire me with the words to express what I believed He had spoken to me through those difficult months.

As I walked down the hallway, I heard Him speak to my soul, saying, "Go back to your prayer space with paper and pencil." I obeyed, asking, "What shall I write?" He told me to draw a heart in the center of the page, but to leave the heart open at the top. After I did that, He told me to draw three rays coming out of the opening at the top, leaving them open-ended. As I did that, I realized that it looked familiar and said, "Lord, this looks like the image of The Sacred Heart". His response was, "No, this is The Holy Heart." As I came to understand, this is an image of my heart and the action of the Trinity as they transform me by Their love, shaping me more and more into Their image.

The Lord continued, "Now draw a rose in the center of the heart with rays of light coming out of both sides of it, for this rose represents Jesus, living in your heart and loving you." After completing that part, He instructed me to draw hands on either side of the heart, and He explained that the hands represent the Father, cradling me in His love. Finally, I was to color the three rays. The center one was to be yellow and the ones on either side of it were to be blue. The yellow ray was to have an arrow drawn pointing down towards the heart. The blue ray on the left was to have an arrow pointing upwards, away from the heart. The blue ray on the right was to have an arrow pointing down towards the heart. He explained that the yellow ray in the center represents the Holy Spirit, who breathes into me His life, love and divine empowering. The blue ray on the right represents the love and prayers bestowed to me by the Blessed Mother. And the blue ray on the left represents the life and love of the Trinity radiating outward to others through my presence, prayers, words, and deeds.

Over the course of time, I grew in my understanding of all that this image means. Two more sections were explained to me: The open space in the heart around the rose represents all the various emotions and feelings that exist in my heart. While they all are a part of the human experience, God wanted me to understand that He wants His peace to reign above them all. And, finally, the space between the hands and the heart represents all the situations and circumstances I experience in life. God is using them all to shape me into the person He created me to be.

Each of the seven sections (labeled A through G) are further expanded and supported by various Scripture verses. These verses were given to me over the course of 10 or so years after receiving the image. Each one, as it was given, was plugged into its appropriate section. It has literally been a learning process, receiving truths that displaced lies, transforming my believing which in turn transforms behavior and living. And that transformation is called growing in holiness. Sections A through E are promises from God's Word that have brought healing, transformation, and freedom. Section F is verses of instruction for living in union with God. And Section G is verses that define the purpose to which God has called me.

It was after reading works by Fr. Thomas Keating that I first learned of the three primary emotional needs of all humans: affection, security, and control. Fr. Keating describes the tendency of mankind to meet those legitimate needs through illegitimate ways such as perfectionism, manipulation, addictions, performance, etc. What I began to realize is that the Holy Heart perfectly corresponds to each of those emotional needs.

Sections A and B address the desire for affection with all its promises of Jesus' love for us and presence within us. Sections C and D address the desire for security with all its promises of the Father's protection and provision. And Section E addresses the desire for control with all its promises of The Holy Spirit's empowering and enabling. And, so, I came to see that The Holy Heart was not just intended for my own personal use, but is in fact applicable to everyone.

This image, and the truth it contains, has shaped me and my relationship with the Trinity for the past 15 years. It is the foundation upon which I build my life, and a framework of truth that teaches me and guides me. Praying with these Scriptures provides a never-ending well of inspiration, and I am certain I will continue to learn from it and be transformed by it throughout the remainder of my life.

THE CREED
OF THE HOLY HEART[1]

- Jesus, I believe You love me. – Jer. 31:3

- I believe You are with me. – Gen. 28:15

- I believe You are in control of all things. – Mt. 28:18

- I believe everything You do is perfect and good. – Ps. 18:30 & Ps. 119:68

- I believe You give me everything I need to live this day and grow in Christ-likeness. – 2 Pet. 1:3

---

[1] Scripture quotes are drawn from The New International Version of the Bible, unless noted otherwise. Many Scriptures have been para-phrased for the purpose of personalization.

9

- I believe I am Your Beloved. – Rom. 9:25

- I believe you accept me. – Eph. 1:6 (KJV)

- I believe I belong to You. – Rom. 14:8

- I believe You make me whole and complete. – Col. 2:10 (NIV & NLT)

- I believe You make Your home in me, and my true home is within You. – Jn. 14:20 & Ps. 90:1 (NLT)

DAILY INTENTIONS
OF THE HOLY HEART

Today I choose:

- To live each moment in union with You, in surrender and trust, receiving Your love and re-gifting it to the world through my presence, prayers, words, and deeds.

- To not take offense, but to see the good in others. If they hurt me, it is due to their not living in union with You. I will forgive them, pray for them, and extend peace.

- To view problems not as hindrances but as gifts. They are opportunities to learn, grow, trust and see Your glory as You take care of everything.

- To practice the ABC's of acceptance:

  A – Allow it to be what it is
  B – Believe that God is actively
      involved in it
  C – Choose to trust that God will
      bring good from it

- To practice thankfulness at all times.

Part 1

"The Promises"

(Sections A through E)

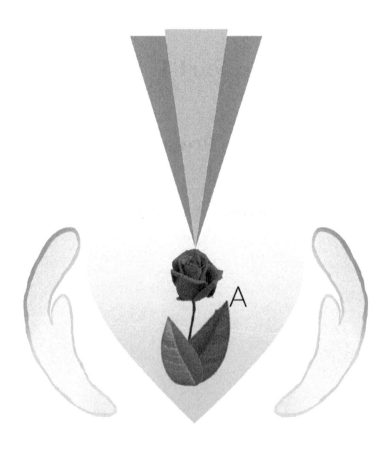

Section A

Because Jesus is living in my heart and loving me, I can let go of my striving for affection and approval and receive instead His loving Presence and acceptance.

Jer. 31:3

**"I have loved you with an everlasting
love, with unfailing love I have drawn
you to Myself."**

*God's love for me never ends or runs out,
can never be stopped or blocked, is always
drawing me home to His heart. His desire
is for me, and His magnetic love is always
pulling me towards Himself.*

Is. 43:1 & 4

"I love you, and you are Mine. You are precious to Me."

God loves me personally. He WANTS me, He cherishes me. While others may not always want me, God always does. My value comes from Him because He declares me to be precious.

Song of Songs 6:3

"You are Mine, and I am yours."

*I belong to Jesus, and He gives Himself
fully to me. We are united, we are one.*

Gen. 28:15

"I am with you and will watch over you wherever you go."

God is my constant companion and my protector. I am never out of His sight.

Jn. 15:4

"Remain in Me and I will remain in you."

God makes His home in me and my true home is within Him.

Eph. 3:17

**"I will be more and more at home in
your heart as you trust in Me."**

*Trust is the key to keeping my heart open
to Him. If I choose to focus on fear, it is
more difficult to experience His Presence.*

Mk. 10:21

"I look at you with love."

I need never fear looking into Jesus' eyes, because He looks at me only with love and compassion, never with condemnation, disgust, or disapproval. An excerpt from "Real Mercy" by Jacques Phillipe states, "In Latin, the word mercy is made up of two words: "misery" and "heart". Mercy is the heart of God that comes to meet every human misery. Jesus looked at Matthew with love, with mercy, a gaze like he had never before experienced. This gaze unlocked Matthew's heart; it set him free, healed him, gave him hope and a new life."

Col. 1:27 (NLT)

"This is the secret: I live in you."

Almighty God, Creator of all things, lives in me. He chooses to make me His temple, His dwelling place, His home. A lifetime is not long enough to mine the riches of this verse, nor are there words sufficient to express its meaning.

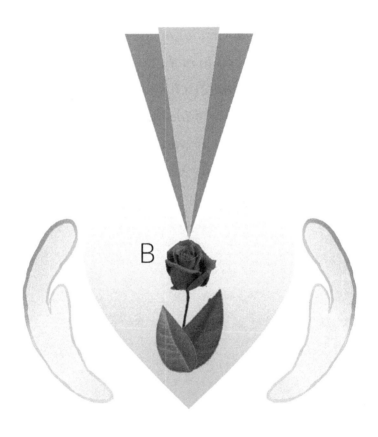

Section B

Jesus wants His Peace to reign over all the various feelings and emotions in my heart.

Ps. 46:10

"Be still and know that I am God."

It is only in stillness and silence that I can truly know and experience God's Presence within me. He never leaves me, but anxiety and fear can cloud my perception of His Presence.

Php. 4:6 & 7

"Do not be anxious, but present to Me your requests with thankfulness and My peace will guard your heart and mind."

No concern is too little to give to God. Thanking Him for what He will do and how He will take care of it is the greatest sign of trust. When I give the burden to Him, trusting and thanking Him, He replaces anxiety with His own peace.

Col. 3:15

"Let My peace rule in your heart."

Many emotions may battle to take charge of my heart, but the choice is up to me ... focus on God and have peace, or focus on the emotion and have turmoil. All emotions are part of the human experience and will be experienced at one time or another. But holding on to painful emotions is like hugging a cactus. Rather than clinging to them, or denying them, or attempting to repress them, it is better to acknowledge them and accept them, then offer them to Jesus and let Him replace them with His peace. No Matter how big the emotion is, God's peace will always be bigger. "May the Lord of peace Himself grant you His peace at all times and in every way (that peace and spiritual well-being that comes to those who walk with Him, regardless of life's circumstances)." 2 Thess. 3:16, AMP.

Is. 30:15

"In quietness and trust is your strength. Rest in me."

Being still and quiet in God's Presence is the only way to find rest for my soul, and it is from that resting in Him that I am strengthened.

Is. 26:3

"I will keep you in perfect peace as you trust Me and keep your thoughts fixed on Me."

Worrisome thoughts are displaced when I focus my eyes on Jesus and choose to trust Him.

2 Cor. 3:18

"As you behold Me, I will transform you more and more into My image with ever-increasing glory."

Spending time in God's Presence lets Him fill me with His light so I can reflect Him in this world. As He transforms me, He sets me free from fear and from self-focus so that I can love others as He loves.

Ps. 34:5

"As you behold Me you will be radiant with joy, your face will never be covered with shame."

Looking to Jesus brings joy to my soul and heals the root of shame deep within that whispers the lies that I am not worthy of love, that I am never good enough.

Ps. 37:7

"Be still and wait patiently for Me to act."

I must not race ahead of God with my own ideas and plans but wait quietly and patiently for His leading.

Ps. 34:4

"I will deliver you from all your fears."

I must not deny, bury, or try to hide my fears, for it is only in accepting them and bringing them to Jesus that He can heal them and set me free.

Section C

Because I am cradled securely in the Father's hands, I can let go of my striving for security and receive instead the Father's protection and provision.

Rom. 8:38

"Nothing will separate you from My love."

God's love is always victorious and nothing can come between He and I.

Jn. 10:29

"No one will snatch you out of My hand."

God will never let me go, no one and nothing can ever take me away from Him.

1 Thess. 5:23

"I am the God of peace who sanctifies you through and through, body, soul and spirit."

It is not my own efforts that will make me holy. I am God's creation, His workmanship, and He takes full responsibility for me. My role is to cooperate with Him by surrendering myself to Him and trusting Him. "Not my will be done, but Thine be done." (Lk. 22:42)

2 Cor. 1:21

"It is I who hold you firm in Christ."

When I feel too weak to hold on to Him, I am reminded that it is actually God who is holding on to me, keeping me firmly rooted in Christ. "All things hold together in Christ, He is the controlling cohesive force of the universe." (Col. 1:17, AMP)

Dt. 33:12

"All day long I shield you, so you may rest secure in My arms."

No matter what I experience in my day, God is holding me through it all. Anything I experience, He experiences with me. Peace and rest come not from having circumstances to my liking, but from having His Presence in the midst of them. "The eternal God is your refuge and underneath are the everlasting arms."
(Dt. 33:27)

Ps. 34:15

**"I see you and My ears are attentive to
your cry."**

*There are times when I do not feel heard
or seen by others. But God always pays
attention to me, He sees me and hears me,
He cares about what I am doing, what I
am feeling, what I am thinking. To be
loved is to be seen and heard, which is to
be validated. To love others, then, is to
affirm their value by being attentive,
making them feel seen and heard.*

Heb. 13:5

"I will never leave you or forsake you."

Friends may come and go, even family sometimes walks away. But God remains always with me, never leaving, forsaking, deserting, or abandoning me.

Lk. 15:31

"I am always with you and everything I have is yours.

Not only does God never leave me, He withholds no good thing from me.

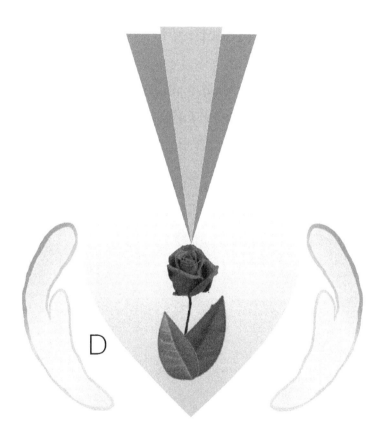

D

Section D

Because God is good, I can trust Him to use every circumstance for my good and to shape me into the person He created me to be.

Rom. 8:28

**"I am using all things for your good
and to draw you closer to Me."**

*God takes everything, no matter how good
or bad it looks, and turns it into some-
thing that is for my ultimate benefit and
to deepen my relationship with Him.*

Is. 14:24

"As I have planned so it will be, as I have purposed so it shall stand."

God is in control, and His Holy Will is guaranteed to be accomplished in His time. No one and nothing can stop it from being accomplished. Knowing His Will is always "good and perfect" (Rom. 12:2), and that He uses everything for good, gives me the peace to rest in His provision, and to surrender my will to His good and perfect will.

Jn. 16:33

"In this world you will have trouble, but be of good cheer, for I have overcome the world."

I can expect troubles and challenges in this life, but I don't have to let them steal my joy because Jesus will be victorious! Every problem has a purpose: to educate me, to grow and mature me, or to allow me the opportunity to serve others. Therefore, problems need not be feared or seen as hindrances, but instead viewed as gifts.

Jer. 1:8

**"Be not afraid of their faces for I am
with you to deliver you."**

*God is with me and helps me to do what-
ever He asks of me. I don't need to look
into the faces of others for approval, or be
afraid of what I might find there, such as
dislike. My desire is to follow God and
obey Him, and I do not need to be controlled by others' opinions and approval.
"Fear of man will prove to be a snare, but
whoever trusts in the Lord is kept safe."
(Prov. 29:25)*

Rom. 8:37

**"I have made you more than a con-
queror."**

*God sees to it that I will not only survive,
but I will thrive. Whatever He calls me to
do, He also enables me to do. Through
Him I am more than a conqueror.*

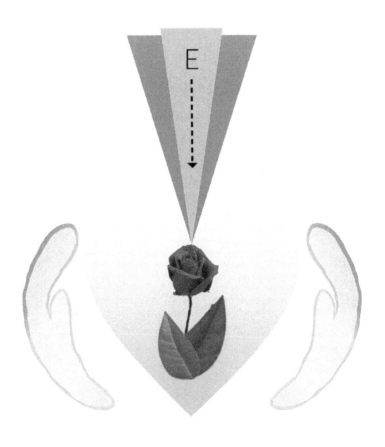

Section E

Because the Holy Spirit breathes into me His very life and love, I can let go of my striving for control and receive His empowering and enabling instead.

2 Pet. 1:3

"My divine power gives you everything you need for life and godliness."

God's Spirit empowers me for whatever I face in this earthly life, along with the power to respond in a Christ-like manner.

Php. 4:19

"I will meet your needs according to My glorious riches."

My needs can never surpass His supply!

Rom. 5:5

"I will enflame your heart with My love."

He satisfies every longing of my heart with His love and fills it to overflowing so that I'm empowered to love Him and others.

Is. 58:11

"I will guide you continually, water you when you are dry and keep you healthy too."

God never leaves me alone and uncertain, without direction. My strength and health come from Him.

Rom. 8:11

"As I raised Christ from the dead, so shall My life empower you."

God's resurrection power is at work within me, enlivening me so I that I am able to participate with His work in the world.

Php. 2:13 (AMP)

"I am always at work in you, energizing you, creating in you the power and the desire to will and to work according to My good pleasure."

God not only helps me to DO His will, He also helps me to WANT to do His will when at times I am tempted to follow my own selfish desires.

Dt. 33:25

"As your days, so shall your strength be."

God's grace is proportioned to my need. No matter how challenging the day, He will provide sufficient grace.

Rom. 8:6

"The mind controlled by My Spirit is filled with life and peace."

When I keep my mind surrendered to God's Spirit, He keeps it peaceful and full of life-giving thoughts. "We have been given the mind of Christ and hold His thoughts, feelings and purposes." (1 Cor. 2:16, AMP) "A calm and undisturbed mind and heart are the life and health of the body." (Prov. 14:30, AMP)

2 Cor. 3:17

"Wherever the Spirit of the Lord is, there is freedom."

The Holy Spirit brings freedom, healing and deliverance to any area that is surrendered to Him. Freedom is liberty from ownership and from that which confines and distresses. He gives me this freedom so that I may live the life for which He has created me.

Part 2

"The Instructions"

(Section F)

Section F

Instructional verses that teach me how to live in union with God so that my heart remains fully surrendered and open, allowing the Holy Spirit to freely live and love through me."

1 Cor. 16:14 & 14:1 (NLT)

"Do everything with love, for love is the highest goal."

God is love and everything done with love is done in union with Him.

Col. 3:17 & 23

"In everything you do, do it all in My name, in dependence on Me. Do it with all your heart as doing it for Me and not for man."

Even mundane tasks, when done in union with Jesus as an offering of love for Him, reaps eternal reward and advances the work of His Kingdom. Remembering that we are working for Him brings joy to the task and frees us from the desire to be appreciated.

Jn. 20:23

"Forgive others and they will be forgiven."

I choose to forgive because I do not want to hinder others from receiving mercy. It is not my job to judge, only God judges fairly and justly. Forgiveness is to give all the negative feelings to Jesus so that He can heal them and so that I will remain open to receiving and giving His love.

Mt. 25:40

"Whatever you do to others, you do unto Me."

I have the privilege of giving joy and love to Jesus when I treat others with love and kindness. But I can also give pain and grief to Him when I treat others with impatience or unkindness.

Php. 2:15

"Do everything without complaining or arguing so that you will shine like stars in a dark world."

Complaining and arguing hinders God's glory from shining through me.

1 Thess. 5:18

"Give thanks at all times."

Giving thanks no matter the circumstance keeps my eyes on Jesus, fuels my faith in Him and keeps me in a place of surrender and trust. No matter what a day may hold, I can always "Give thanks to the Lord, for He is good, His mercy endures forever." (Ps. 118:29)

2 Cor. 5:17

"Live by faith, not by sight."

No matter how things look, I will choose to trust.

Prov. 12:18

"Reckless words pierce like a sword but the tongue of the wise brings healing."

Words live on in minds and hearts for a lifetime and have the power to give life or bring death to the soul.

1 Cor. 10:31

"In whatever you do, even eating and drinking, do it all for My glory."

Every single action can be offered to God for His glory, nothing is too small or insignificant.

Col. 4:2

"Devote yourself to prayer, being watchful and thankful."

This is the highest calling: a life of prayer, being attentive to God's Presence, expressing trust through thankfulness. Being watchful entails understanding that whatever circumstances I am faced with, they are only a story within a story. God is using the circumstances to create a greater story. Part of being watchful, then, means to look beyond what I see with my eyes, looking instead with eyes of faith at what God is doing, and cooperating with His will through trust, worship, and gratitude.

Part 3

"The Call"

(Section G)

Section G

The love and prayers of the Blessed Mother, in whose footsteps I am called to follow.

Mary the model, Christ the center.

2 Cor. 9:8

"I am able to make all grace abound to you so that in all things, at all times, having all that you need, you will abound in every good work."

God's grace is constantly streaming to me, much like ocean waves rolling onto the shore, wave upon wave. "For from His fullness we all have received, grace upon grace." (Jn. 1:16)

Mary's example: She was full of grace – Lk. 1:28

I will choose to receive His grace in all things and at all times.

Gen. 2:7 & Jn. 20:22

"I breathe into you My very life."

Every breath and every heartbeat reminds me that God is filling me with His Spirit, His very life.

Mary's example: She received the Holy Spirit and conceived Jesus – Lk. 1:35

I will allow myself to be filled with His life and Spirit.

Mt. 13:58 & Eze. 22:30

"I am unable to do many miracles in your land due to unbelief ... will you stand in the gap between Me and your land? Will you believe?"

Yes, Lord, I will answer Your call, I choose to believe in You and in all You can do. Jesus, I trust in You.

Mary's example: She believed – Lk. 1:45

I choose to believe and trust.

Heb. 13:15

"Through Jesus continually offer praise to Me by proclaiming His Holy Name."

The Name of Jesus is exalted above all things (Ps. 138:2), and to lovingly speak His Name is the greatest prayer I can offer. The Catholic Catechism states "The invocation of the Holy Name of Jesus is the simplest way of praying always ... it is possible at all times because it is not one occupation among others but is the only occupation: that of loving God, which animates and transfigures every action in Christ Jesus." (CCC 2668)

Mary's example: She praised the Name of Jesus – Lk. 1:49

I will let the Name of Jesus become a constant prayer within me.

2 Cor. 1:3

"I hold and comfort you in all your troubles; be a channel of My comfort to others."

All of God's love and mercy, everything He is, flows not just TO me, but also THROUGH me, as He blesses others by living and loving through me.

Mary's example: She offered comfort by taking the needs of the couple at the wedding at Cana to Jesus, and by taking John as her own son there at the foot of the cross in the midst of her own suffering. (Jn. 2:1-11 & Jn. 19:25-27)

I offer myself to God as His channel of comfort, inviting Him to live and love through me.

Epilogue

The image of the Holy Heart depicts a glorious truth. God, in the form of Father, Son, and Holy Spirit, makes His home in each and every person. The Holy Heart is not just a one-dimensional drawing of a spiritual concept. It is a truth that is alive and living within us. God lives in us all. He loves us all. He is alive and active in us, desiring to draw us into ever-deepening union with Himself. We all are the Holy Heart. Some of us have not yet realized this. Some of us struggle to believe it. And those of us who do believe it are all at various points on the lifelong journey of transformation and union as we learn to cooperate with God's grace, which is always working within us.

God's mercy and grace do all the work of freeing us from sin, healing our wounds, softening our hearts, opening our eyes and ears to the truth, giving us the faith to believe, enabling us to love even as He loves, and so much more. Our part is a simple one … surrender and trust. Surrendering ourselves to His love and to His will, trusting in His love and His goodness as He leads us moment by moment through our days.

What we speak of here is not just the journey of a lifetime, but the relationship of a lifetime. I pray that in reading this book your eyes have been opened to the truth that all of us are The Holy Heart. May your heart be awakened with fresh desire to open yourself more fully each day to the Father who gave you life, the Son who gave His life for you, and the Holy Spirit who gives you life anew.

69382205R10056